OWD TOM — A CYCLING LEGEND

Albert Winstanley, was born in [...] in 1916. Formerly employed [...] aircraft technical clerk, his main pastime since the age of 16 has been leisurely cycling. Together with his active pen and camera, since 1930, he has toured extensively throughout the British Isles, Norway, France, the Spanish Pyrenees and Ireland.

For many years he has been a prolific contributor to periodicals and newspapers, and during the 'social season' devotes much time lecturing to clubs and organisations about his 'wheeling' adventures.

In April, 1966, at the age of 50, Albert became eligible to join a unique organisation known as the 'Autumn Tints Cycling Comrades'. As a member he was privileged to hear fascinating tales told by 'old timers' about the founder, 'Owd Tom' Hughes. Convinced that the story of 'Owd Tom' would be of interest to cyclists and non-cyclists alike, and that his name should rightly occupy a permanent place in the history of British cycling, he began to research the facts. The result is this fascinating true account of *Owd Tom — A Cycling Legend*.

OTHER TITLES BY THIS AUTHOR:

The Golden Wheels of Albert Winstanley
(1985).
ISBN 0 86157 162 2.
Countryside Publications
(out of print).

Golden Days Awheel (1991).
ISBN 0 9514333 9 3.
Owl Books

Owd Tom
A Cycling Legend

by
Albert Winstanley

OWL
BOOKS

First published June 1992
by
Owl Books
P.O. Box 60,
Wigan WN1 2QB

ISBN No: 1 873888 15 5

Designed and produced by
Park Design and Print, Wigan.

Text produced via high resolution DTP
in 11.5 on 13pt Palatino.

Printed and bound in Great Britain

Contents

Foreword

THE reflections and remembrances met with down the 'road of life', are precious and, perhaps, personal. Stored in the memory are the many 'milestones' that have marked the way. Those that are worthy of being kept alive should be shared with others. That is why, in these our retirement years, my good wife Evelyn and myself, treasure the memory of the Unicorn Cafe and Tearooms of Walton-le-Dale, the home of my parents, Fred and Annie, from 1901 and latterly our own home until 1978.

The 'Unicorn' is still there, just around the corner from our present home, though it is now under another name, which, perhaps, in this modern age, is considered more in keeping with the role it now has to play.

The reflections and remembrances of our long stay there embrace, among others, the memories of that amazing and unique cyclist 'Owd Tom' Hughes and the 'Autumn Tints Cycling Comrades' he founded.

It is fitting that the many 'milestones' from his own cycling 'road of life' should have been gathered together and captured in the chapters of this book.

Evelyn and I consider it an honour to have been requested to supply the Foreword and in conclusion we hope that the many 'Veteran' cyclists who knew 'Owd Tom', or knew of him, will, as they read the chapters, bask once again in the reflected glow of those 'golden years' of cycling.

In addition, to all those approaching the 50th 'milestone' of their own lives, we would both say: "Remember 'Owd Tom', and join the 'Autumn Tints Cycling Comrades'. By so doing you will enjoy priceless friendship, companionship and pleasure".

George Fletcher
Evelyn Fletcher

This book is dedicated to those 'Veteran' Members of the 'Autumn Tints Cycling Comrades', who knew 'Owd Tom' Hughes; those who know of him, and those who will now learn about him.

Acknowledgements

THE little task I set my pen to perform and fulfil has been done, but the chapters could not have taken shape without the valuable help and assistance I received from so many old and new friends who had expressed their interest and wished me success in the venture. It is to them I should like to acknowledge my appreciation and thanks, as follows:

To the many 'Veteran' and 'Senior' members of the 'Autumn Tints Cycling Comrades', who supplied a vast collection of photographs and press cuttings relating to Owd Tom, for me to pore over and select from.

To three of Owd Tom's grandchildren, who so courteously invited me to their homes to share the recaptured memories: Mrs. Edna Cottam, of Whitley, Wigan, who told me of Owd Tom's last days; Mr. Frank Malley, who produced for my inspection treasured memorabilia of his grandfather; and particularly his grandson of the same name, Mr. Tom Hughes, of Standish, near Wigan. On my several visits to his home I received lovely hospitality, and I was readily given permission to photograph anything I wished relating to his grandfather. He also patiently checked the chapters of the manuscript regarding names, dates and events I have mentioned and also kindly contributed the most interesting article: 'Some Notes and Hints on Riding The Penny-Farthing Bicycle' on p.95.

In addition, I should also like to express thanks and appreciation to:

The Editor of *Cycling World* for permission to include as Chapter 11, the article previously published by them; the Editor of the *Wigan Observer* for permission to reprint the 'Obituary' in Chapter 12; George and Evelyn Fletcher of Walton-le-Dale (stalwarts of the old 'Unicorn') for regaling me with so many tales and stories of the past; The Staff of Rivington Hall Barn, for allowing me to photograph at my leisure 'The Tom Hughes

Chair', and who so kindly continue to keep it well polished; Herbert S. Williams, of Maghull, Liverpool, for assistance received.

In conclusion may I thank the Publisher, Alan Roby of Owl Books, for his interest, editing and presentation of the text and illustrations.

Introduction

CHERISHED memories and recollections are wonderful things as they contribute to the precious quality of one's life. They are stored in the mind for later reflection in idle moments — particularly in one's advancing years.

Memories and recollections are manifold and cover many aspects of life; from childhood to adult days, bringing pleasure and comfort in advancing years. Included are the pursuits and pastimes one has indulged in over the years.

My own cherished memories and recollections are of a lifetime of cycling and cycle-touring, and the happiness it has given and is still giving to me. They include too, the friendship and fellowship that has radiated with membership of numerous cycling clubs and outdoor organisations I have belonged to. Such membership began in the exuberance of my first teenage cycling years, when I began to capture the magic of cycling.

One day came a day in my cycling life, when, perhaps with a feeling of 'dread', I had attained my half century. I was fifty years old and eligible to become a member of a most unique and honoured cycling organisation: The 'Autumn Tints Cycling Comrades'. I received my badge of membership, with my name engraved upon its scroll and pondered on the silent message of the badge — a tree shedding its autumn leaves.

At the foot of the tree was a monogram — the intertwined initials 'T.H'. They were the initials of Thomas Hughes, the Wigan founder of the Autumn Tints. From that day onwards, I have been honoured to have been a member, and today I wear my badge with pride.

Unhappily I was never to meet Tom Hughes personally, but throughout my continued membership and the years that followed, his name was to become a legend, and I was to hear amazing stories, tales and anecdotes about him and his wonderful contribution to the world of cycling.

I realised that these were memories and recollections of a much admired and loved man, and that they should never be forgotten.

They were worthy of being gathered and collected together, before it was too late and preserved in book form. I decided that the 'shedding autumn tree' of the badge, was akin to my own advancing years, and I would accept the little task of preparing such a compilation, before it was too late for me to do so.

This then is a book about the memories and recollections of Tom Hughes, or 'Owd Tom' as he preferred to be known, and the 'Autumn Tints Cycling Comrades' he founded.

In compiling and writing it, my own cycling wheels have turned many times to the haunts and places he loved and revered, where his name is still remembered. They have taken me also on visits to many 'old timers' and veterans of the wheel who knew and respected him, and who with a gleam in their eyes have related their meetings with him, and of the pleasures of the 'golden age' of cycling, particularly with the Autumn Tints.

Innumerable photographs, newspaper cuttings and extracts linked with 'Owd Tom' have come my way. All of them are a tribute to the high esteeem everyone regarded him with.

I trust, therefore, that as you turn the pages of what follows, that my humble pen may help to radiate and convey the happiness of the good things 'Owd Tom' left behind as a rich inheritance to the delights of cycling.

Albert Winstanley
Bolton, 1992

Opposite: *Thomas ("Owd Tom") Hughes (1866-1950). Founder of the 'Autumn Tints Cycling Comrades'.*

1

Early Days

"Oh, to be in England"
Browning

TRY to visualise the Lancashire countryside, in the spring of 1866, a day that typified the words of Browning. The poet was then alive, capturing word beauty with his gifted pen; Queen Victoria was on the throne and Britain was at the zenith of its colonial powers.

Countryside Lancashire was never more beautiful. Patterned fields, flower-sprinkled hedgerows, and small villages enjoyed a delightful picturesque quality.

Life was at a more leisurely pace; the horse was king of the road. Travel between our villages and towns was still largely undertaken on horseback, or by stagecoach or on foot, but the horse was being challenged; bicycles were then on the road and had been for 26 years. Ever since that day in 1840 when Kirkpatrick MacMillan, a young Scottish blacksmith, had invented the very first bicycle by ingeniously attaching 'treadles' to a 'hobby-horse' type of wooden frame.

There was to be rapid development of the invention and a firm favourite type of cycling machine of the times was the 'Ordinary'. To give it its affectionate title — the 'Penny-Farthing'.

Now you may very well be asking why I have chosen the year

1866, to give this picture of Lancashire. The answer is because in that year, to be precise, on the 21st of July, at Salford, Tom Hughes was born. Little realised his proud and approving parents that their son was destined to become one of England's most famous cyclists, and that his name would always be held in high esteem, and is still a legend to this day.

Following his early days in Salford, the family moved first to Durham and then to Wigan. Tom started work at Garswood Hall Colliery, near Wigan at the age of 11, and was a coal miner for 54 years.

A lovely Penny-Farthing now comes onto the scene, a 'thoroughbred' built in 1874, and 52 inches tall. On it, Tom began cycling in 1887. "In Queen Victoria's Jubilee Year", he once stated.

There is a picture of proud Tom, taken on 21st July of that year,

Proud Tom, aged 22, in 1888.

standing with this machine, He looks quite 'dapper' and wears typical cycling dress of that age, sports a cap and a collar and tie. There is a large button-hole in his lapel, and he also wears a watch with an 'Albert' chain from his pocket. His cycling shoes look strong and sturdy, and are polished and shining.

This Penny-Farthing was to be his favourite machine, and 50 years on there are a few celebration photographs of him riding the very same bicycle. Each suitably captioned with one of his many humorous quotations: "May your tyres hold their breath and your breath never tire", "When going up the hill of prosperity may you never meet a friend", "Life beaut (without) fun is summer beaut sun". A seasonal greeting is additionally given: "A happy landing for Xmas", or "A merry Xmas, Keep Smiling".

Owd Tom, aged 72, in 1938.

2
Clubman, Trackman, Tourist and 'Mile-eater'

TOM was to be a club cyclist all his life. The first local club he joined was the *Pemberton Cycling Club*, near Wigan, and he was made the club captain in 1888. It was a very popular club, and we see him on a photograph of club members taken in 1894. The photograph is a wonderful reminder of the pleasure of cycling in those days, and the high 'safety' bicycle is much in evidence. Moustaches were then the fashion of the day — only six members appear to be clean shaven. There is a wide selection of various types from the 'walrus' to the 'thin upper-lip'.

A favourite place to wear the club badge was on the hat, and they are very well placed there. There is a sprinkling of bowler hats and most members are wearing collars and ties.

Tom is there, with a handkerchief peeping out of his breast pocket, holding the handlebars of the youngest member of the club, who is standing next to him

Like many young cycling men of the day, he was 'bitten' for a short spell by the 'speed bug', and enjoyed a season of track racing. He won a mile scratch event, and came second in another race.

In an interview of remembrances in 1940, he referred to his 'track' days, saying: "I found I could get more fun out of touring,

18

Pemberton Cycling Club 1894. Tom Hughes (seventh from left) became Club Captain in 1888.

and chucked the speed work in favour of it".

It was also during this interview, that he revealed he had told a lie about his age when he was eleven, stating he was twelve, to enable him to start work in the mine.

His amazing will-power and determination was revealed, when he said: "I had only three days at school and prior to my marriage it took my sweetheart the best part of three months to teach me how to write my name, so that I would be able to sign the marriage register".

In spite of his lack of formal education, the flair for writing was there and he developed a natural gift to describe, to advantage, what he saw on tour with a good deal of penmanship.

He joined the well-known *Wigan Wheelers* in 1919, and also became a member of the *Cyclists' Touring Club*, and began to tour extensively throughout the British Isles, France, Belgium, Germany and Italy. He particularly enjoyed Switzerland. In 1943, on a reflection of the miles he had covered, he estimated it at 400,000.

From 1926 to 1941, he recorded his miles, and over the 16 years the total was 149,136 miles. For four of the years, he topped 10,000 miles a year. There is an unfortunate gap in the records between September and December 1931, with the simple explanation: "Run down by motor cycle — broken leg etc."

This cycling chart also shows, he had extended the places he had toured, to Lands End to John O'Groats and Ireland (four times), Isle of Man, Isle of Wight and Bavaria. His fame was growing and he began to be recognised throughout England. Indeed, it is stated on good authority, that a letter addressed to:"Tom Hughes, Cyclist, England", reached him safely in Wigan.

Down the years, cycle touring has been the perfect medium for friendship, fellowship, and companionship, no matter what one's calling, and how refreshing it is to read, of a little memoir of Tom's that reflects this perfectly: "I have often cycled abroad, including a visit to the Passion Play at Oberammergau. Last year

TOM HUGHES' 16 YEARS CYCLING CHART. MONTHLY AND YEARLY TOTALS.

YEAR	1926	1927	1928	1929	1930	1931	1932	1933	1934	1935	1936	1937	1938	1939	1940	1941
JAN.	508	803	500	565	680	656	83	731	701	644	409	582	615	445	388	511
FEB.	539	537	345	462	759	553	215	584	690	634	662	548	892	516	245	531
MAR.	671	816	516	628	985	674	537	798	781	1013	803	602	772	717	828	828
APR.	779	1020	829	803	923	461	1108	951	799	760	923	816	952	824	670	888
MAY	1237	1029	901	859	1205	1188	841	987	1329	950	1000	1068	937	987	785	1120
JUN.	1409	1528	1520	877	910	911	879	1335	1256	1540	838	852	1069	788	909	972
JUL.	1115	1045	993	1318	774	1372	1142	1068	861	874	1122	891	805	725	745	1161
AUG	731	628	689	721	1150	135	791	871	865	972	1166	927	903	785	843	966
SEP.	618	814	992	719	656	RUN DOWN BY MOTOR CYCLE	624	811	794	925	659	968	782	782	705	940
OCT.	705	841	718	740	723		751	687	619	624	802	888	701	590	700	789
NOV.	587	550	537	639	693		684	734	626	624	670	788	749	691	672	877
DEC.	719	638	906	772	656		577	622	740	563	630	514	721	780	764	887
YEARLY TOTALS	9616	10147	9446	9103	10094	5950	8242	10179	10061	10123	9684	9440	9698	8630	8253	10470
CUMULATIVE TOTAL		19763	29209	38312	48406	54356	62598	72777	82838	92961	102645	112085	121783	130413	138666	149:36

TOM HUGHES STARTED CYCLING AT THE VICTORIA GOLDEN JUBILEE 1887.
FROM 1926 TO 1942 HE HAS CYCLED 148,790 MILES, WHICH INCLUDES— LANDS END AND JOHN O'GROATS,— IRELAND 4 TIMES,— ISLE OF MAN,— ISLE OF WIGHT,— BELGIUM,—GERMANY,—BAVARIA,—FRANCE,— ITALY—AND—SWITZERLAND.

Owd Tom's Mileage Chart from 1926 to 1941 records that over 16 years he achieved 149,136 miles, and for four of the years he topped 10,000 miles a year.

I had a cycling trip to France, Italy and Switzerland with a Master of Arts, and a Foreign Office official for companions. I then cycled over the Alps and one night slept 4,500 feet up".

This amazing man, who had to be taught to write his name for his marriage, was to be admired for his determination and courage. His exceptional stamina and love of cycling was a glowing example of the perfection of the life he was living and enjoying.

3

Memories of the Unicorn

I AM hoping readers will not mind if I introduce this chapter with a fiery and tempestuous story in English history — a true story that even today, almost 350 years on, still bears witness to an outstanding military strategist and ruthless adversary that was once Oliver Cromwell. Although the story has nothing whatsoever to do with cycling, the setting of the finale, when revealed, most definitely has!

The year is 1648, and King Charles I sits on a 'shaky' throne and rules over a most unhappy England. Cromwell, the Lord Protector of England, one of the most colourful figures of our island's history, and his Puritan army, have been engaged in the Civil Wars.

In that year, at Preston, Cromwell was engaged in a fierce battle that would change history. It was the 'Battle of Ribbleton Moor'. The climax of the battle took place at Walton-le-Dale, where the River Darwen unites with the Ribble.

Cromwell was a brilliant strategist and planned the campaign carefully — after all, his army was smaller than that of Hamilton's Scots.

Cromwell had carefully reconnoitred the terrain and had

noted the meeting of the two rivers. In a brilliant manoeuvre he drove the Scots towards it, cutting off all means of retreat. Then the carnage began, so much so, that both rivers ran red with blood. The poet Milton was to perpetuate the memory of it all with his line: "Darwen stream, with blood of Scots imbrued".

Today, at Walton-le-Dale you can still see the hill down which Cromwell chased the retreating Scots; its grim name is still retained as 'Butcher Brow'.

After his victory, Cromwell returned to the village inn which had been his headquarters when planning the battle, and the name of the inn was the 'Unicorn'. It is still there, though now languishing under another name, and I shall tell you of its treasured memories shortly.

We are told that the day after the battle, there was a large 'pay parade', where Cromwell stood in one of the downstairs rooms of the inn, and paid his men their dues 'battle wages', handing out the money from an open window.

For many years there was a memorial plaque on one of the outside walls of the Unicorn, recording the battle; it had been placed in position by the Cromwell Association and I was pleased I was able to photograph it before it was taken down.

A reminder of the Civil War in Lancashire is Butcher Brow at Walton-le-Dale, near Preston, where Cromwell chased and slaughtered the retreating Scots.

* * * *

To thousands of cyclists, particularly those of 'veteran' years, the mere mention of the 'Unicorn' will bring a sigh of pleasure and nostalgic tears to the eyes, as memories are rekindled of what surely was one of England's most famous cyclists' 'tea places'.

The Unicorn Inn was already heavy with centuries of old memories, when in 1901 it was taken over as a cafe and refreshment house.

There are lovely old sketches and photographs of the Unicorn at Walton-le-Dale, when our roads and lanes were virtually traffic free. Most certainly Tom Hughes with his 'terrier-like nose' in seeking a cyclists 'Mecca' would have been one of the early regulars, sampling the wonderful hospitality of Mr. and Mrs. Fred Fletcher, the proprietors. Throughout Tom Hughes' lifetime, the Unicorn would be managed by the same family. George Fletcher, their son, who was born there in 1907 was to take over on his father's death in 1953, and continued to do so for 25 years.

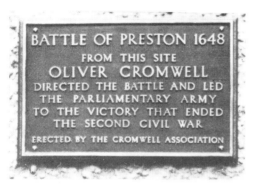

To commemorate the Battle of Preston in 1648, this plaque was once located on a wall of the Unicorn, Walton-le-Dale. Being the place from where Cromwell directed the battle and afterwards paid his men their dues.

Today, George and his wife Evelyn, are retired but it has been my good fortune to have called upon them on several occasions, at their Walton-le-Dale near Preston, home — only a 'stones-throw' away from the Unicorn, — they have often regaled me with lovely stories of the past.

I have been a ready listener when George has told me stories of his teenage memories under the watchful eye of his dad:

"My early days were taken up with the interest of the customers — people in horse-drawn carriages etc. We had three stables and other outbuildings. 1914 brought the war, but after the war more and more cyclists came on the roads, and regular groups seemed to keep together. *Continued on page 26*

The Unicorn, Walton-le-Dale, near Preston, as it appeared before the turn of the century and (below) as it was in the 1960s. As the Unicorn Cafe and Tea Rooms for decades it was a cyclists' 'Mecca' until it closed in 1978 on the retirement of George and Evelyn Fletcher. It was here on 12th July, 1924, that Owd Tom Hughes founded the 'Autumn Tints Cycling Comrades'.

George and Evelyn Fletcher of Walton-le-Dale, were the proprietors of the Unicorn from 1953 to 1978.

> "I remember Tom Hughes and his pals — always in mid week and on Sundays — calling. This was when they formed the section and called themselves the 'Autumn Tints Cycling Comrades'".

This important event in cycling history was made on 12th July, 1924, and I find it so easy to picture in my mind's eye, the proceedings. I feel sure they went something like this:

> Tom Hughes (In the Chair):
> "Neaw Lads, we're aw gerrin' owder, but eawr cycling's gerrin' better and better, an eawr 'appiness shud be shared wi' others. Heaw abeaut us formin' a club fer chaps and wimmin like us and cawin' oursels 'Th' Autumn Tints'. We'll 'ave a badge, wi' a tree on it, wi' its leaves fawin'".

Naturally, the 'motion' would be carried unanimously, and so the 'Autumn Tints Cycling Comrades' was founded.

Also present on that momentous day were Tom Gray, George

Taylor ('Old Gabriel'), the Lock Keeper and Toll Collector from the Leeds to Liverpool Canal's Top Lock, Wigan, and Jack Parr. All of them were also members of the well known *Wigan Wheelers Cycling Club*.

Tom Hughes was then 58 years old, but the eligible age for joining was to be 50, just as it is today ... and this, mark you, was to be the 'junior age' of membership. On reaching 70, members would achieve 'senior' status.

A most interested listener to the proceedings on that day was the late Arnold Hall ('Pegasus') from Wigan, who in later years would acquire fame and skill as a photographer and cycling journalist.

Recapturing his own memories in 1978, when he wrote regretfully of the closing of the 'Unicorn', 'Pegasus' left a fitting description:

> "To us of The Autumn Tints, the closure of the Unicorn would be a great wrench, for our organisation was born there one sunny day in 1924. I listened to Tom Hughes making the inaugral speech, little thinking that fifty years on I would propose the toast of 'The Founder' at the Jubilee Dinner, and that I would join them in 1950. In pre-war years, Wigan Wheelers held their annual New Year's Eve party at The Unicorn. Many times from there I set the wheels rolling at 11.45 p.m., leaving the party, to ride the old year out and the new year in. The bells of Preston greeting those new years were a joy to hear; would I could hear them again in similar circumstances. Still, as my wife says: 'You have done those things, and have the memory of them forever'".

From those early beginnings the 'Autumn Tints' just grew and grew. The Unicorn was to be the 'Mecca' of their regular meetings, but there also were to be other cyclists tea places — Rivington, Halton, Frodsham and many more, where meetings would take place.

Mention too must be made of the vast collection of curios and oddities that could be seen at the Unicorn, for George Fletcher's father was an avid collector. There was the 'Unicorn Lion' with its beady eyes, that occupied a prominent place in one of the rooms. George related a few stories about it, especially as the two animals were linked:

"The Lion and the Unicorn were fighting for the crown,
The Lion beat the Unicorn all round the town,
Some gave them white bread, and some gave them brown,
Some gave them plum cake, and drummed them out of town".

There came the time when the Unicorn Lion just had to go. He was getting a bit 'tatty' and was occupying too much room. The Lion found a new home on Blackpool Promenade, and formed a prop for visitors to be photographed with.

Sometime afterwards, a group of cyclists calling at the Unicorn remarked to George: "Ee, do you know that lion you had — well we've seen it in Rhyl". Tom Hughes and the early Autumn Tint members knew it well; it was a firm favourite.

Many of those 'old-timers' of the cycling world, and especially Autumn Tint members will recall those pre-war days, as the 'golden age' of cycling with that irresistible joy and freedom of the open road. The English countryside was then a sheer delight of little lanes, so peaceful and tranquil. There were numerous village cottages that offered teas and refreshments, and where the kettle was always on the hob. There was fellowship and comradeship on the club run, a cheery "Hello" to the cyclist who passed by, and every day awheel was an exciting adventure.

On 21st July, 1936, a most important event had occurred in the history of the Autumn Tints. Tom Hughes had reached the year of his allotted scriptural span. He was seventy. Now eligible to become a Senior Member. From that date onwards, he would be affectionately known as "Owd Tom" Hughes.

4

Oil, Acetylene, Pint Pots and 'Butties'

On a sunny Sunday morning not long ago, I stood on the spacious car park behind Pinocchio's Italian Restaurant and Pizzeria in Walton-le-Dale. My cycle was parked by a wall of the restaurant, and I was alone, save for a dog who bounded towards me for a friendly pat.

Standing there in the silence of the morning, a thousand memories tumbled from my mind. The memories were lovely ones, yet all were tinged with a touch of sadness. What I was looking at was the former Unicorn Cafe and Tea Rooms, now under a new Italian title. But then, these are the years of the final decade of the century, and I suppose the new name suits the new clientele.

It is said that cycling nostalgia for the past should not be indulged in, for the clock certainly cannot be turned back. I am a romantic, however, who loves to recall the halcyon days of cycling, just as I am sure there are other veterans of the wheel, particularly those of the 'Autumn Tints Cycling Comrades', who are also romantically inclined. To them and to me, the Unicorn, as we knew it, will always hold a precious niche in the memory, for we shall never see the likes of such old cyclists' catering establishments again.

How well I recall my early fledgling years as a cyclist in the pre-war years of the 1930s. Times were hard and our pockets were light. Our bicycles were like carpets of magic, transporting us to delightful countryside days. It was 'heigh-ho' for the freedom of the open roads and was a phase of life we thrilled to, with the ever-present genial companionship of fellow clubmen, the laughter and the good-natured fun.

The Lancashire lanes, the fell tracks and bridle-ways of the Yorkshire Dales and the Lake District, all unfolded their beauty to our wheels. Then there would be the homeward ways, and the wonderful atmosphere of the many 'tea-places' that abounded in those days, which catered so well for the cyclist.

It was the age of the Lancashire pint pot of tea, laced with as much milk and sugar as you desired. There was none of the dolls-house size cups, the silly small packets of sugar, and the plastic sachets of milk, in vogue today. No, from the pint pot, you could drink long and deep and give a satisfied . . . A-a- ah. Then with 'butties' unpacked you ate them in the good company of fellow clubmen.

Everyone had a favourite tea-place but there was one to which we returned again and again — the Unicorn.

As I stood there on the empty spacious car park behind 'Pinocchios' on that Sunday morning, indulging in past memories, I just had to relive again a typical day out with my fellow club cyclists, and tea at the Unicorn:

> The club run had been to the popular Trough of Bowland; the tang of autumn was in the air. We have experienced the wild joys and ecstasies of being with these Bowland fells, and the lanes of Wyresdale have been lovely in the afternoon quietness. The A6 highway has been reached via Scorton village; there has been a fast ride to Preston and the thrill of the steep drop down to cross the Ribble to reach Walton-le-Dale.
>
> As we swing into the yard behind the Unicorn, every inch of wall space is occupied by a 'festoon' of bikes, and ours are added to the mass. We open the door to a packed room and a hub-bub of cyclists voices. There is a continual 'coming and going' as Mr. and Mrs. Fletcher are busy carrying trays of pint pots of tea, and

Mr. Fred Fletcher (father of George), in the kitchen of the Unicorn. He was an avid collector of antiques and curios, all of which delighted the many cyclists who called for refreshment since he became proprietor in 1901.

plates of food. A cheery coal fire burns in the grate, protected by a sturdy fireguard. This homely atmosphere is reflected by the other contents of the room. You look at curios collected over the years: stuffed animals, the nose of a swordfish on a wall, a framed auctioneer's advertisement for the sale of a 'church pew', also a notice telling that "This establishment will be closed for the day, due to the funeral of Queen Victoria".

It is 'lighting-up' time when we leave. The wicks of oil lamps are being cleaned with matchsticks, and acetylene lamps are being primed and we each indulge in the ritual. For weeks I had been saving hard, and was the proud owner of a new acetylene lamp and as happy as the proverbial 'sandboy'. I open the glass, and turn on the water. A sniff at the burner, tells me the gas is coming through nicely. Then I strike a match and hear the sharp 'plop' as the gas ignites and the lamp burns with a mellow glow.

It was an age of the oil and acetylene lamp (although battery lamps were around); the cycle dynamo was still in its infancy.

In those fledgling days at the Unicorn, I often met and spoke to the 'old timers'. To me, they were men of experience, leisurely in their ways, yet with still eager eyes, and unbounded enthusiasm for cycling. Little did I known then that these were the men of the Autumn Tints. There was one among them who radiated happiness, bounding with energy, and with a weather-tanned face . . . it was Tom Hughes. Little also did I know that 30 or more years on, I too would become a 'Tint', helping to keep alive the wonderful spirit generated by Owd Tom, in this continuous saga of cycling.

The noise of a motor car engine roused me from reverie . . . my dream is ended as the car swings into the car park and I realise it is 1992 again. I wheel my bike away from its parked place; there is something I have to do. I have to ride to the junction of the A6 highway to its meeting with Walton New Road. I shall ride the short distance to the house where George and Evelyn Fletcher, the last proprietors of the Unicorn live in their retirement. There will be coffee and cakes. George, now 83, will tell me more stories of the early days of the 'Autumn Tints' and of that day of 12th July, 1924, when Owd Tom Hughes founded it.

5

Friends and Comrades

THE formation of the 'Autumn Tints Cycling Comrades' brought about a wonderful sense of friendship and comradeship that was to prevail throughout the years. The 'veteran' cyclist, who had reached the 'autumn' year of 50, could meet companions of either sex. Cycling was now for joy and at a leisurely pace, and lifelong friendships would result.

I am sure, it was Owd Tom's finest hour, and that he was experiencing a feeling of inner happiness with others sharing in the spirit of it all.

One of the earliest members, who had been a constant companion of Tom's, was George Taylor, Lock Keeper and Toll Collector of the Leeds to Liverpool Canal's Top Lock, New Springs, near Wigan. Their friendship lasted for over 20 years. George Taylor was to become known as 'Owd Gabriel', who was often to report under this pseudonym the "doings" (as he put it) of the 'Autumn Tints', in the *Wigan Observer*.

He often indulged in poetry writing, which he composed in a jocular vein. A verse listing a conditions of membership of the 'Autumn Tints':

" Autumn Tints."

Founded by TOM HUGHES, July 12th, 1924

HE who is enrolled in this unique club must be either grey or bald,
   At the least he must be fifty, yet at a hundred he's not too auld.
There must be silver in his hair for him to come up to the scratch,
But he is allowed a fringe of greyless hair if the top is void of thatch.

The ladies, God bless 'em, may be registered at fifty years of age,
Provided they can stuff an old bird with unions and sage,
For the old cocks of the north need women to look after 'em,
So they'll keep the men correct by persuation or stratagem.

—Owd Gabriel.

The Two 'owd uns' were to appear together on many photographs. I like the one taken in 1929, showing them side by side behind the village stocks at Warburton on the road to Lymm, Cheshire. As a background there is a beautiful white thatched cottage. Tom has printed a Christmas message on the photograph: "There's gladness in remembrance".

Often They indulged in the most hilarious of 'leg-pulls', especially in their correspondence with each other. I have a letter written in 1942 by Owd Gabriel to Owd Tom reminiscing on their friendship of 20 years. "20 years interesting peregrinations", as he so aptly states. It is addressed to Tom, as "Satan, Prowling About, Birch Street, Wigan":

> "Owd Tom Hughes is as mad as a March hare
> If he's made an appointment and isn't there
> The slower speed in wind is carefully calculated
> He faces every milestone as he has Tabulated.

"It was a broiling summer day in July 1922, when I met Satan on Downham Brig. That was 20 years ago. He did not look so much of a Devil as he does now. Had he curled the ends of his moustachios, A-La-Kaiser, Mephistopheles would have been his understudy. Coming down to recent times, Owd Tom puts me in mind of hollow-eyed Ribbentrop, and placid Molotov, signing an eternal pact of friendship between the two nations, while Stalin was looking over their shoulders, looking as 'fauce' as Old Nick himself. Tom and Joe shake hands ... both of you are Imps of the Devil, up to all kinds of Divilment"

The letter continues reminding Owd Tom of how he had lured him on a Hundred Mile Ride:

"On nearing home, did you not add insult to injury, when I slithered in an icy rut, and lay there like a German soldier freezing to death in Russian snow ... not caring a damn how the world goes by. The while you were laughing with fiendish glee at my discomfiture".

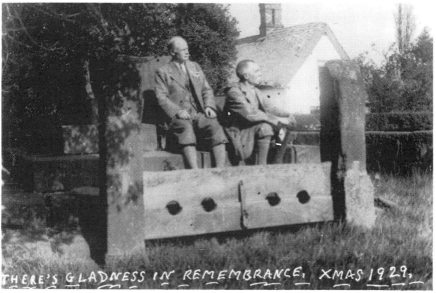

George Taylor (left) and Owd Tom near Lymm, Cheshire, in 1929. George was Lock Keeper and Toll Collector of the Leeds to Liverpool Canal's Top Lock, New Springs, near Wigan. The pair were good friends for over 20 years.

When Owd Tom's arduous occupation of the work-a-day week in the mine, and then to "lure" his companion on a hundred mile ride for relaxation is considered, his great stamina and fitness and his love of cycling can truly be appreciated.

Often in those days, Autumn Tint members enjoyed their attempts at poetry. Granted there were no Keats, Shelleys, or Wordsworths among them but their verses rang with a homely quality and often in the Lancashire dialect — more popular then than it is today.

In June 1937, we find Autumn Tint member Albert Hardman from Leigh, composing lines about some of the members:

AN APPRECIATION OF 'OWD TOM"

If e'er yo' get howd o't paper,
Especially t'Cycling News,
I'll gamble yo'll find i' some corner
A few words abeaut Owd Tom Hughes.

He knows every shire i'th country
He's travellin' every day,
An' whenever yo' happen to meet him,
I'll warrant he's lively an' gay.

'Wigan Wonder' Ben Adhem used t'call him
An' he's noan so far off bein' reet
For a chap as can do his 'ten thousand',
At his age, it's no little feat.

To those that have'nt a bike
My advice is to get one to-day
Use it weel, an' make it a pal
An' the doctor yo'll not need to pay.

It gets yo' eaut into th' country
An' keeps yo' fro' feelin' so blue
If you deaut me, just ax Mr. Goodwin
An' the young jockey's but '82'.

It'll noan wear yo're beef off, don't worry
It'll make yo' hearty and strung,
Why! look at eaur '16 stone champion'
Jack Olding, as broad as he's lung.

But neaw I mun close this short poem,
An' wish th' Autumn Tints aw the best,
An' when we've aw' finish eaur ridin,
We'll be thankful to lay deawn an' rest".

Cycling octogenarian and 'Tint' member was the late John Charnock of Bolton. John was cycling until the age of 89 years and died at the age of 93 in 1967. His 'Song Of The Veteran Cyclist' is stirring stuff and gives short shrift to complaining old men and the "bogey of three-score and ten":

SONG OF THE VETERAN CYCLISTS

You will meet, now and then, with some elderly men,
Who are spleeny, decrepit and sad,
Who are prone to remark that the future looks dark
And the universe all to the bad.
So they bungle along, with their livers all wrong
And the sense of the average hen.
Let them speak for themselves and go lie on their shelves,
They're not our type of elderly men,
No, not our type of elderly men.

Chorus
(To the glorification of elderly men,
Let us dedicate our salutations again,
Ignoring the bogey of three-score and ten,
May they flourish for ever and ever, Amen)

Some elderly chaps may be eighty, perhaps,
Well, they're sixty, we'll say, at the least
And they think it disgrace if they hadn't the pace
Like the lightning sufficiently greased.
Over fell and thro' dale, they ride without fail,
To the haunts of the curlew and wren.
Happy years on the wheel have left sinews of steel
In the limbs of these elderly men,
Yes, these ever-young elderly men.

Then here's to the elderly men,
To their valour and vigour and vim,
To their wisdom and wit, which have failed not a bit,

To their soundness of wind and of limb.
May their friendships be faithful and firm,
Every ill be remote from their ken,
May their zest in the game be for ever the same,
"Three times three", for these elderly men
(By gosh!)
Yes, these valiant elderly men.

In extreme contrast, is a poem by Charles Lee, which demonstrates to perfection, Owd Tom's deep love of the countryside. His was a simple but satisfying joy and appreciation of nature, as he pedalled along with good companions to share it with. The raptures of the four seasons; the songs of birds, the murmur of a river or a moorland stream, the scent of blossom-laden hedgerows and fragrance of flower-filled meadows.

It was cycling at its very best, and he would take the memories with him on his work down the mine, happily charged with the knowledge, it would all be there again for him to savour, the next time he was 'awheel'.

I think Charlie Lee's poem — A Bit of Heaven, sums up Owd Tom's feelings:

A BIT OF HEAVEN

Owd Tom, once declared in an interview that the village of Erbistock-on-Dee was "a little bit of heaven".

I met a bluff old collier
A-cycling through a vale
His sparkling eyes and merry smile
Told their own unvarnished tale;
I listen'd to his stories
Recited with much glee,
Of the marvels and the mysteries
Of scenes unknown to me.

After listening, thrilled, entranced
By all that he had told,
I was borne away to dreamland
By old Collier Tom the bold;
Swiftly cycling on he led me

Past scenes of tree and rock,
to that little bit of heaven,
Known to all as Erbistock.

Then he, with bright and twinkling eyes,
Clear as the sky above,
Said: "Friend, there is no place so fair
As this village which I love".
Here, gazing on the silvery Dee,
Flowing from its place of birth,
You may sit and dream quite happily
At this fairest place on earth.

6

The Photographic Jester

PERHAPS you have never been to see Maggoty Johnson's grave, perhaps you have never even heard of him! If not, do let me acquaint you with a most fascinating story, that is enshrined in a woodland grove, near Gawsworth, in Cheshire.

Maggoty Johnson's real name was Samuel Johnson (not the famous one), and the name "Maggoty" was bestowed upon him by the locals of the area some 200 years ago. His eccentricity was manifested in his wish to be buried in unconsecrated ground and to have a little cemetery all to himself. He died in 1773.

Maggoty Johnson was the last 'jester' of England. He was employed to entertain at several large manor houses before the gentry, particularly at nearby Gawsworth Hall. One of the famous characters he played, was that of Lord Flame. He assumed this name when on his travels — giving instructions that due reference was to be made of it on his gravestone. The grave gives its own story:

> Stay thou whom chance directs or ease persuades
> To seek the quiet of these sylvan shades:
> Here, undisturbed and hid from vulgar eyes,
> A wit, musician, poet, player, lies:
> A dancing-master, too, in grace he shone

And all the parts of op'ra were his own;
In comedy well skill'd he drew Lord Flame,
Acted the part, and gained himself the name.
Averse to strife, how oft he'd gravely say,
These peaceful groves should shade his breathless clay,
And when he rose again, laid here alone,
No friend and he should quarrel for a bone;
Thinking that there some old lame gossip nigh
She possibly might take his leg or thigh.

Before me, as I write, I have a very old photograph, and it must be some 60 years old. On it are three cyclists: 'Owd Gabriel' (George Taylor), Owd Tom Hughes and Percy Wellings — three members of the Autumn Tints. They are sitting together on top of Maggoty Johnson's grave, and the more I look at it, the more amusing it becomes. Owd Gabriel having made a point, points his pipe towards Owd Tom Hughes, and I am sure the conversation went something like this:

Owd Tom indicating the grave beneath him is saying:

"By gum, yon mon wi bein a jester, mun a bin a reight card, wot wi' 'is music, dancin, an' aw them theer jokes".

The grave of Maggoty Johnson 'the last Jester in England'. He died in 1773 and is buried, as he requested, in unconsecrated ground, near Gawsworth, Cheshire.

Left to right: George Taylor, 'Owd Tom' and Percy Wellings at Maggoty Johnson's grave in the early 1930s.

Owd Gabriel answers:
"What art talkin' abeaut. He were nobbut moor a jester than thee, wi' thi' 'Tum Foolery', and aw that trick photography".

Owd Tom: "Aw reet, aw reet, but yon Maggoty, wud a med a reight gud un, in eaur 'Tints', wot wi his lowfin (laughing), jokes and wit, and I'll warrant he wud a fair danced on't pedals".

I am sure the conversation flowed with such good humour, and that Maggoty's glade at Gawsworth rang with the homely quality of Lancashire dialect.

Meanwhile Percy Wellings sat on the extreme edge of the grave had regarded the two 'owd uns' with a quiet nonchalance, after all he was used to their friendly banter, especially as they had been cycling together for over 20 years.

To me, it is a happy picture. I could not agree more with Owd Gabriel, for it brings to mind the photographic "doings" that Owd Tom delighted in, during his long years awheel. His camera was always a faithful companian, and just like a jester, he loved to share his enthusiasm for photography with his friends and fellow clubmen.

From his first cycling days of 1888, there is a photographic cartoon of him. He is seen holding a 'mongrel' type of bike with exaggerated balloon tyres. It carries the title of "The favourite (Swank)".

Everyone loved the 'double' photographs he became skilled in, and we see him and his 'double' holding a tandem, the caption reads: "Them 'Hughesful Twins' ready for the road". There is also a 'racing' photograph titled "Veterans Race", with the two Owd Toms ready for the off, among others.

His interest in photography was kindled during his early cycling days, and throughout his life his enthusiasm never faded. Those early years were the days of the heavy plate cameras, and Owd Tom was a noted and popular figure with his camera slung over his shoulder.

He also enjoyed to give his 'Magic Lantern Shows'; his favourite subjects being countryside views, as well as local beauty spots and he also had a large collection of noted personalities he had met. One man he met during the early years

Continued on page 47

The photographic jester. From his early cycling days, Owd Tom was interested in photography. Everyone loved the 'doubles', at which he became highly skilful. The photographs on this and pages 45 and 46 show that his humour, manifested in his photography, was never far away.

THEM HUGHESFUL TWINS READY FOR THE ROAD.

NEAW TOM. THRUTCH.

DUMPING RUBBISH AT LOMRO GREEN.   14.10.3?

VETERANS RACE

TOMMY AND FRITZ,

TOM HUGHES LIKE JOHNNY WALKER
—STILL GOING STRONG
AS HE WILL APPEAR IN THE
WIGAN CARNIVAL
July 11TH 1931

Thirty-two years separate these two photographs and the event. Owd Tom as he appeared at Wigan Carnival in 1899 and also in 1931.

of his stage career was George Formby senior, the creator of the 'Wigan Pier' joke. Owd Tom was privileged to take photographs of George in his stage 'gear'. In 1904, George Formby junior was born and Owd Tom was a frequent caller at the family's home at 3 Westminster Street, Wigan, and is credited with having taken a very early photograph of George Formby junior, at the age of five years old, and sitting on a donkey.

Just as Maggoty Johnson dressed and performed the part of a jester, imitating Lord Flame, so was Owd Tom to dress and imitate a well known personality everyone knows. It was the occasion of the Wigan Carnival on July 11th, 1931. Owd Tom is dressed as the famous 'Johnnie Walker' Whisky symbol . . . 'Still Going Strong', and he rides a 'hobby-horse'.

He was then 65-years-old, and smiling as much as ever.

Hundreds of Wiganers applauded him as he trundled his 'hobby-horse' along, doffing his top hat and acknowledging the waves of the crowds. He was to have the last laugh out of that little episode; for the photograph was forwarded to the world famous makers of the whisky. Owd Tom received from them, as recognition and appreciation . . . a crate of whisky.

7

Tom the Family Man

"TWENTY-ONE" was once a most important day in the life of most men. It was the age of full maturity, when the traditional 'key of the door' was handed down from one's parents as a 'symbol of manhood'.

It was so with Tom Hughes when he achieved this status in 1887. Cycling had not claimed all of his leisure time, for he had come to meet and court Alice Ann Cartwright. In addition to returning his affection, she had very capably and determinedly taken him 'well in hand', proving to be a most efficient teacher in the difficult task of teaching Tom to read and write. He was to be a determined scholar under the tuition of Ann, although it was to take three months before he could, with efficiency write his name. This would be essential, because on 21st May, 1888, Tom and Ann were married at Pemberton, near Wigan, and Tom had to sign his name on the marriage register. Alice was then 22.

The marriage was No. 310 in the Parish of Pemberton register, and is recorded on page 153.

Those were the years of large families and Tom was to become the father of three sons, and five daughters. They were Ted, Tom, Bill, Sally, Bertha, Polly, Alice and Nellie.

Proud Tom and Alice with their first baby.

Owd Tom and his family in 1938. Back (left to right): *Sally, Edward (Ted), Tom (jnr), Bertha.* Front: *Mary (Polly), William (Bill), Alice, Owd Tom and Nellie.*

A photograph taken in 1938, when Tom was 72, shows him with his family, and at that time he had 22 grandchildren. Unhappily his wife was not on the picture as she had died in 1928 at the age of 61.

The name 'Tom' bestowed on one of his sons, was still further to be carried on to his son also. It was indeed, a pleasure when I was invited to call at the Standish, near Wigan, home of Owd Tom's grandson. During the several hours together, we browsed over old family photographs, and I was also shown other visible links with 'yesterday'.

The first was the marriage certificate, and then two old medals were produced, that had been found in a purse many years ago. They recalled Owd Tom's working days in the mines. The first was inscribed 'Lancashire and Cheshire Coal Owners Association' and it depicted the Red Cross, a pick and shovel, a wheatsheaf and the Lancashire Red Rose. The reverse was inscribed 'Awarded to Tom Hughes 1913'. The other medal was for St. John's Ambulance War Service, and depicted the Red Cross, and the Cross of Saint John's, and was inscribed on the reverse: 'Tom Hughes 5179. 1914-1919'. It was an award for ambulance service work during the First World War.

Owd Tom's three sons were to become accomplished cyclists, especially Tom junior, who was the youngest. He was to acquire international fame, and with different partners the following records would fall to his own and to his partners' wheels:

Liverpool-Edinburgh. Tandem Bicycle - 1925 with T. Ibbison
London-Liverpool. Tandem Bicycle - 1926 with J. Sheppard
Liverpool-Edinburgh. Tricycle - 1927
Liverpool-Edinburgh. Tandem Tricycle - 1920 with A Hughes (a
     cousin).
Edinburgh-York. Tandem Tricycle - 1928 with Eric Robinson

In 1929, seeking financial support and sponsorship, he was

Owd Tom and sons about 1920. Left to right: *Tom (Jnr), Edward (Ted) and William (Bill).*

Tom Hughes in 1991 (grandson of Owd Tom) with his grandfather's medals associated with his days in the mines, St. John's Ambulance War Service and the 'Autumn Tints Cycling Comrades'.

given a tricycle by the firm of James (a well known make at that time) and on this machine, he broke the Lands End-John O'Groats record, completing the distance in 3 days 21 hours and 55 minutes. The tricycle was equipped with a single 'free-wheel'.

Small wonder Owd Tom was as pleased as proverbial 'Punch' at the successes of his son.

There was a lovely photograph of Tom the grandson, taken when he was about nine years old, sitting on his father's tricycle, with Owd Tom looking benignly down at him.

I was readily given permission to photograph anything I was interested in. As I did so I could not help comparing the photography of today, with those years, when Owd Tom was cycling with his camera as a companion. On his cycling travels he carried a heavy plate camera on his back, even on his many tours abroad. He did his own processing and made hundreds of glass slides, that formed the subjects of his many 'magic lantern' lectures. Many slides were produced for my inspection, and they were a veritable 'open sesame' to a fascinating social history.

From Tom the grandson, I was also to learn about what would later become the well-known cycle firm of 'Tom Hughes, Cycle Dealer and Lightweight Specialist'.

It all began when Tom Hughes junior had completed his

apprenticeship as a fitter in 1925, and had been handed his first week's wages as a journeyman. He was then told that as "things were bad", he should "go on the dole" for a few weeks, and "we'll send for you, when things buck up". In those days, this was a polite way of getting the sack; the practice was widespread.

Tom Hughes junior at Lands End on 21st June, 1929, at the start of his Lands End-John o' Groats record-breaking attempt on a tricycle. It took him 3 days 21 hours and 55 minutes.

Tom started to do bike repairs in his mother's back yard, and made such a success of the venture that he branched out, making it a business that flourished. Eventually it resulted in the well known shops, that even today are spoken of with affection by veterans of the wheel.

Though Owd Tom had no connection with the business, he would be a frequent visitor, especially in his later years, when he had to give up cycling altogether.

There was a moment during my meeting with grandson Tom that I shall always treasure. It came when I was handed a badge of the now familiar 'Autumn Tints Cycling Comrades' . . . but on the scroll of this one was engraved the name of 'T. Hughes'. In my hand was the number one badge of the 'Tints' that had been worn by this amazing man who had begun it all. That badge must be preserved to keep alive the spirit of fellowship that he had fostered, and so cherished by veterans of the wheel today.

Right: *Three 'Toms' and three generations. Owd Tom with his son and grandson in 1943.* **Below:** *"Owd Tom's Gang" is title of this happy family gathering taken in 1941.* **Back row:** *(left to right) Uknown, Harry Myers (grandson), Polly Myers (daughter), Bertha Hurst (daughter), Alice Malley (daughter), Sally Griffin (daughter), Ted Hughes (son), Bill Hurst (grandson), Jenny Hughes (grand-daughter — now Parkinson), Frank Malley (s-in-l), Tom Hughes (son).* **Front:** *Alf Myers (s-n-l), Dorothy Hughes (s-n-l), Ann Hughes (d-in-l), Tom Hurst (grandson), Owd Tom, Arthur Griffin (grandson), unknown, unknown, Tom Hughes (grandson), Elsie Hurst (now Clayton) (grand-daughter), Arthur Griffin (s-n-l).*

54

Left: *Owd Tom smiles approvingly at Tom, his grandson, who is 'trying out' his father's tricycle in the early 1940s.*
Below: *"Tom Hughes" was the name of this cycle shop in Mesnes Street, Wigan taken in the mid-1950s. The sole proprietor was Tom Hughes junior. Pictured in the doorway is Tom junior's son (also named Tom) with his cousin Harry Freeman. The shop existed at a number of locations in Wigan from 1925 to 1970, when it was sold to Oliver Somers, an existing well-known local trading name.*

8

Life Begins at Seventy

"The days of our years are
three score years and ten; and
if by reason of strength they
be fourscore years, yet is their
strength, labour and sorrow; for
it is soon cut off and we fly away"
Psalm 90 Verse 10.

THERE are many who cannot repress a shudder when the dreaded verse from the scriptures becomes linked with their lives. For many also, it becomes the age of the armchair and slippers, and patting the grandchildren on the head. A recall of days of long gone by are related, and all that has been done and achieved in life.

"Fiddlesticks", I say. Seventy is the beginning of a new age, especially in the life of a dedicated cyclist.

Golden days are ahead waiting to be enjoyed and relished. If you have not got a bicycle, spend some of that 'nest egg' put away for a 'rainy day' and join the ranks of the Autumn Tints Cycling Comrades. You can bask in the radiated friendship and fellowship of other seventy-years-old men and women of the 'Tints', and you can, above all, hear and learn about what Owd Tom Hughes did when he became seventy, who equally said "fiddlesticks" to the verse of the Psalm.

Owd Tom had now reached 'Senior Status' in the ranks of the 'Tints'. There was so much to do — more meetings for the Senior members, birthday parties to be arranged, particularly at the Unicorn at Walton-le-Dale, where Mrs. Fletcher would bake those huge mouth-watering cakes, to be ceremoniously cut.

First of all, such an important day in his life had to be celebrated awheel. We see him astride a new cycle with gleaming slightly dropped handlebars, complete with the very popular 'Lucas Challis' bell. In position is the school satchel draped over the top tube to hang in the triangle, in which to carry his touring essentials. To record his future miles, the cycleometer is there too. His face glows with good health, and is smiling at this, another 'milestone' in his life. The photograph is titled: "Tom Hughes — 70 today, 21.7.36".

Five days later, his birthday was celebrated at the Unicorn, Walton-le-Dale, and what a wonderful occasion it was. Seventy or more members were there to honour him, and to display their esteem and affection. He is now officially "Owd Tom" having acquired and achieved 'Senior Membership' of the *Autumn tints Cycling Comrades*, and we see him smartly dressed in cycling attire, wearing a rose in his buttonhole.

Mrs. Fletcher of the Unicorn had baked and decorated a superb

An exhilarated Owd Tom astride his new bicycle on his 70th birthday.

57

Owd Tom cuts the customary birthday cake on 26th July, 1936, five days after his 70th birthday. Having then achieved 'Veteran' status of the 'Autumn Tints Cycling Comrades'. Other 'Veteran' members look on with eager anticipation.

cake, a two tier one, and Owd Tom steadies the bottom layer as he deftly cuts into the top one.

His many fellow members and companions beam their approval and give a spontaneous ovation. There was also to be a lovely surprise for Owd Tom on this the celebration of his seventieth-birthday — the presentation to him of an illuminated address to express the regard and esteem for him by members of the 'Tints'.

Moving on from that day in 1936, may I ask readers to join me on a sunny afternoon, 55 years later, when, after lengthy enquiries, I finally found out where the illuminated address

---

Opposite: *The Autumn Tints Cycling Comrades and father and sons (Bill, Ted and Tom junior) celebrating Owd Tom's 70th birthday. On the occasion Owd Tom was presented with an illuminated address, expressing the high regard and esteem for him by fellow members.*

'TUMN TINTS' CELEBRATING TOM HUGHES'S 70th BIRTHDAY. 26.7.36.

could be seen. That afternoon, I called at the home of Frank Malley, a grandson of Owd Tom, the son of Alice, one of Owd Tom's daughters.

Frank lives at Whelley, Wigan. After parking my bike there was a ready invitation to enter Frank's home, and a mug of coffee appeared in a twinkling. I found him to be full of enthusiasm for cycling, having toured extensively, both by tandem and solo. Together we chatted and relived memories of Owd Tom, and looking at many old photographs. Then the illuminated address was produced for my inspection.

Frank Malley, grandson of Owd Tom Hughes proudly displays the illuminated address in 1991 which was presented to his grandfather on his 70th birthday, 55 years earlier. (See p.59).

As I admired the beautiful calligraphy, I found it to be a moving moment. It was delicately decorated with a surround of colourful leaves and bordered in gold, and was complete in a matching gilt frame. Its text and message read:

"Presented to Mr. Tom Hughes,
otherwise Owd Tom of Wigan,
by the members of the
Autumn Tints Cycling Club,
on the occasion of the celebration of his
70th Birthday,
at The Unicorn, Walton-le-Dale
on Sunday, the 26th July, 1936.

A slight token of their love and esteem for him, and with their
sincere thanks for all he has done for the club since its
inception

And with the hope that he may long continue to be an
outstanding example of what consistent cycling will do to
keep a man fit and enable him to get the best out of his life".

"Snows may o'er his head be flung
But his heart, his heart is young"
Tom Moore

I feel sure these carefully chosen words caused tears to flow
from Owd Tom's eyes as the illuminated address was presented
to him, and I am equally sure he would have been overcome by
the ovation of his many friends and fellow members on that
memorable day at Walton-le-Dale.

Frank, laughingly, also produced a unique memento of Owd
Tom's link with his Penny-Farthing days; a miniature model of
one that had been presented to him in 1940.

The model was only a few
inches high, but it was a veritable
masterpiece of workmanship. It
was mounted on a small crate
which could be opened to
ingeniously house it. The four
sides were labelled "Exclusive
Design" "British Throughout"
"Tom" "The Swift August 1940"
and "Owd Tom Hughes, Wigan".
The front wheel was a penny, and
the small rear one a farthing
dated 1860. The 'penny-farthing'
actually worked, with tiny rubber
pedals to turn the front wheel,

*In the home of Frank Malley, is this
unique memento of his grandfather's link
with the Penny-Farthing bicycle.*

61

and there was even the tiny footrest in position by which those old time cyclists mounted their machines.

Owd Tom's seventieth birthday and the following celebration at Walton-le-Dale was a wonderful occasion, and demonstrated to perfection the comradeship and fellowship which prevailed in cycling circles, particularly to those veteran members of the 'Autumn Tints Cycling Comrades'. Many more birthdays would be celebrated, not only for members who had attained 70 years, but onwards.

* * * *

Tom Moore's verse was a well chosen one, not only for Owd Tom's illuminated address, but for those grand old men (not forgetting the sprinkling of ladies) of the Autumn Tints of 1936 who were to demonstrate that life did begin again after seventy.

Looking at the now fading photographs that have come my way, happiness shines throughout all the regular meetings and the birthday celebrations.

Owd Tom is on most of them, his nut brown face laughing and smiling his contentment. Depicted are the many cycling haunts that were firm favourites those days, just as they are popular venues for cycle runs today. There is Bolton-by-Bowland, Downham, Wycoller, Trough of Bowland, Lymm, Pickmere, Frodsham ... and a host of others. Every run seems to have been photographed by some member of the party to include Owd Tom in the picture.

The birthday 'meets' were attracting large gatherings, and there are pictures at Rivington, Halton Castle, near Runcorn, Parbold, and Ribchester. The Unicorn, Walton-le-Dale was, however, to remain the favourite — particularly because of Mrs. Fletcher's by then traditional birthday cakes. In many photographs we see her beaming her approval, as the all-important 'first cut' is made and then later to be sliced into pieces and shared around.

Attending one of these birthday meets was a young cyclist

from Bolton I knew very well. His name was Tom Higham. Tom had vivid memories of the occasion, particularly as it took place on one of his first cycle rides.

He had been invited because "he would get a piece of cake". But the climax, and the meeting with Owd Tom would be something he would never forget. He told me his story: "I went to Walton-le-Dale and I got a piece of cake, and met Tom Hughes. In fact he rode part way home with me, and said: "Dost know .. . thas geet same initials as me 'T.H'. When tha grows up, tha mun join th' Autumn Tints". Little did Owd Tom realise that the young cyclist riding by his side was later to become a future Secretary of the Autumn Tints, who would serve well and keep up the traditions for 19 years.

The fame of Owd Tom had by now spread nationwide, and several of the noted cycling journalists of the day were coming to meet him. Among them were 'Kuklos' and 'Wayfarer', whose writings are still spoken of with reverence.

CYCLING "SEVENTIES"

Brave the Gale To Honour Their
Oldest Member

Veteran cyclists from Lancashire and Cheshire, members of the Autumn Tints Cycling Club, attended the 80th birthday party at Halton, near Runcorn, Cheshire, yesterday of Mr. H. R. Goodwin, of Manchester, their oldest member.

Despite the boisterous weather the veterans cycled between 30 and 40 miles to attend the party.

Mr. Tom Hughes, of Wigan, founder of the club, refused an invitation from the B.B.C to take part in the "In Town To-night" feature in order to be present.

The Autumn Tints Cycling Club is one of the most exclusive organisations of its kind in the country.

To become a member a cyclist must have reached the age of 50. After reaching 70 the member is accorded a birthday party.

'Cycling "Seventies" brave the Gale to Honour Their Oldest Member', was the headline of a news item in October 1935, when 'Autumn Tint' members gathered at Halton, near Runcorn, to celebrate the birthday of their oldest member, 80-years old Mr. H.R. Goodwin, of Manchester. His wife, 72, also a member, is on the right. Owd Tom and others helped to make it a good day.

Mention the Lancashire dialect and the name of Teddy Ashton (Allen Clarke) will be recalled. He was a Bolton man who moved to Blackpool around 1912 and was a 'down to earth' Lancastrian and countryside lover. In addition to his popular Lancashire dialect tales, his literary talents were to become famous through Windmill Land — the story of the windmills which in those days were widespread throughout the Fylde.

Teddy Ashton was to become a firm friend of Owd Tom and around the year 1920 they were often to be seen cycling the Lancashire lanes. There is a photograph of 'Teddy' and Owd Tom "On the road to Wembley 9th August, 1924". Both of them are on 'roadster' bikes, Teddy on a high 'sit-up-and-beg' model, where he has his mackintosh strapped to the handlebars. He also wears a 'homburg'; both wear collars and ties and both have the usual 'Albert' watch chains, snaking to a waistcoat pocket. Tom has his indispensible school satchel draped from the top 'tube', and the oil lamp is in position as is the favourite 'Challis' bell.

To me, this photograph is the perfect portrayal of a dedication to cycling — the pedalling to London on roadster machines, and with both riding 'single freewheels'. When I showed this photograph to a good cycling friend of mine, he remarked: "They don't make men like that today!"

Owd Tom's dedication to the Autumn Tints was also to be demonstrated on a birthday celebration held on a day of high winds and drenching rain in October, 1935. The occasion was the birthday of the then oldest member, Mr. H.R. Goodwin of Manchester.

It was held at Halton Castle, near Runcorn, in boisterous conditions. The veteran cyclists had pedalled the 30 to 40 miles to get there. Owd Tom is seen smiling as usual in the photograph that was taken. Yet perhaps the smile hides a touch of disappointment. At that time, one of the most popular of Radio Programmes was "In Town Tonight", with celebrities attending the studios of the BBC to record their stories for the nation.

Owd Tom had received an invitation to take part in the programme, which unfortunately was on the same day as the

*Firm friends! Teddy Ashton,
Lancashire dialect writer and
Owd Tom were often seen
cycling the Lancashire lanes
together in the 1920s. Below
they are pedalling to
'Wembley' on 9th August,
1924. Teddy on his 'roadster'
sit-up-and-beg is wearing a
'homburg' hat with
mackintosh strapped to his
handlebars. Owd Tom is on
his 'roadster' with dropped
handlebars. Both are wearing
collars and ties.*

birthday celebration of the Tints oldest member. When he could quite easily have been in a warm studio, rather than disappoint his cycling friends, he braved the gales and lashing rain to honour the oldest member of the Tints, and turned down the BBC invitation.

It was in the true spirit of the 'Autumn Tints Cycling Comrades', and a display of friendship and fellowship at its very best.

9

Laughter and Sadness at The Bike Shop

IN these my own veteran years, when passing a well stocked cycle shop, I still find it impossible to resist peering into the windows to see what is on offer, and to look at all the latest 'gadgetry' of this modern cycling age. My word, what a modern age it is too, with 'multi-gearing', ultra lightweight and carbon fibre frames, disc wheels, computers on the handlebars, hi-tech lighting systems, and a host of other refinements.

I am equally sure it was the same with Owd Tom Hughes, when he was in his son's shop. As he approached his 'eighties', his legs were beginning to tire and there he could browse with nostalgia for his early Penny-Farthing days. I have looked at many Hughes family photographs in recent times, and several in his later years; he is seen with a walking stick. When I called on his eldest grand-daughter Mrs. Edna Cottam, she told me much of the sadness that was to come during his last years.

His son's shop was a wonderful place for him to escape to, to live and dream his memories of years past, and to see everything around him linked to cycling.

Many veteran members of the Autumn Tints still recall the shops, often meeting Owd Tom there, in his latter years.

Into this saga of Owd Tom Hughes, may I now introduce a veteran Autumn Tint member, and a gentleman of the tricycling fraternity, who during his younger years was a frequent visitor to the cycle shop when it was located in Wallgate, Wigan. His name is Jim Healey. Jim hails from Hindley on the outskirts of Wigan and has a broad Lancashire accent developed by being brought up in a mining community and for many years working in the pit. To be in his company is a unique Lancashire experience.

I laugh when I recall a meeting of a cycling organisation I belong to, when under the item of 'any other business', Jim rose to his feet to speak. Immediately the Chairman asked for an 'interpreter' to 'translate' for him. Owd Tom too was a dialect man.

Autumn Tint Veteran, Jim Heeley, of Hindley, near Wigan, was a frequent visitor in his younger days, to the Wallgate bike shop. There he recalls Owd Tom's dialect humour and sometimes "caustic" tongue.

Though Owd Tom had kept up-to-date with the evolution of the bicycle, and had adapted himself accordingly to all the improvements that took place, he always retained that fondness for the Penny-Farthing; especially as it had been linked with his first days as a cyclist

His son had acquired a lovely model which was kept at the Wigan, Wallgate, shop, and there was an occasion when Jim Healey called, and Owd Tom was enthusing about its qualities. Suddenly Owd Tom turned to Jim

At the time the photograph was taken this particular Penny-Farthing was owned by the old gentleman with a moustache and wearing a flat cap who is stood by the rear wheel. The machine had been very expertly restored for its owner and Tom junior told the owner that he would like to buy it should it ever be for sale. Some time later it was sold to Tom junior and was used by him on several occasions. It was kept at the Wigan cycle shop and eventually sold to someone in America for £25. At the time it was more than the cost of any new bicycle in the shop. It was on this machine that Jim Healey took up a challenge by Owd Tom to "have a do on it".

and said: "Bet tha corn't ride it", "Bet ah con", said Jim. "Aw reet", said Owd Tom, let's see thi; goo on, 'ave a do on it".

Jim chose a convenient wall to gingerly mount the machine, and set off in good style, with Owd Tom laughing and cheering him on. Slowly Jim mastered the art and was enjoying the experience and did a few circuits, Then he began to worry, knowing he would have the problem of stopping and "Gerrin off". He shouted to Owd Tom: "How do a ger off". Owd Tom in fiendish glee replied: "Same bloody road tha geet on". Poor Jim had to rely on slowing and seeking the support of the wall, before tumbling in a heap with the bike on top of him.

When Jim told me this story, he added: "An' I scrawped aw mi arm on't waw".

I was told later that when the Wallgate shop closed, the Penny-Farthing was sold to an American "to show the folks back home!"

There were times too when Owd Tom could sport a 'caustic' tongue. On one occasion when Jim was in the shop a young disappointed-looking boy came in holding a tyre, together with its inner tube, showing a large cut in them. He handed them to Owd Tom, and asked if they could be repaired. Owd Tom looked at the tyre and tube and said: "Th' only road ud be to get a new un". The young boy said he could not afford a new tyre and tube, whereupon Owd Tom replied: "Well it'll be chep-per for thi t' get a new tyre and tube in't lung run than t' tee five peaund o' sausages reaund thi wheel rim neaw."

Jim also mentioned an occasion when he was cycling to Walton-le- Dale, and passed Owd Tom, who had up-ended his bike and had the rear wheel out. Jim shouted: "Con ah 'elp thi Tom", as he pedalled slowly by, at which Owd Tom replied: "Dost think a corn't mend mi own puncture?"

There was, however, to be the sad day when Jim was in the shop talking to Owd Tom's son. Suddenly Tom looked through the window and in an alarmed voice said: "There's Dad, and he's 'all over the road'. Owd Tom was now approaching 80 years of age and was beginning to become a danger to other road users in still trying to cycle. Very quickly they got Owd Tom back into the shop, with the pretence of showing him something to interest him. Unknown to Owd Tom his cycle was taken out of his sight and dismantled. It was the end of Owd Tom's cycling days, and despite his pleas, for his own safety he was never allowed to cycle again.

10

The 'Tints' Carry On

FOLLOWING the death of Owd Tom Hughes, there was a short period in the 'doldrums' for the 'Tints'.

In 1951, George E. Haigh of Newstead, Halifax, took over the Secretaryship, and regular meetings were maintained, particularly at Walton-le-Dale, Rivington, Parbold, Lymm and Denshaw.

George became a well known and popular figure, and was also known as the "Man in the White Cap", this being his favourite head-gear. George was to serve the Tints so well for a period of 14 years, until his death on 23rd September, 1965, at the age of 71.

Before 1965 had ended, Ben Booth of Middleton, near Manchester, was appointed Secretary, and the membership was growing fast. There was a flourishing East Pennines Section also holding regular meetings. A glance at the programme of those years, reveals Hope, Shepley, Wharncliffe Side, Woodlands and Langsett being their favourite venues. There was also a Section in East Anglia holding monthly meetings.

The year 1966 was an important one, for it marked the 100th anniversary of the birth of Owd Tom Hughes. In this year also, it was decided to hold a dinner at the Rivington Hall Barn, and this was so successful it was to become an annual event.

I am fortunate to have in my possession several of the printed menus and 'Toasts' cards of the Dinners held during the 1960s and afterwards — all of them autographed by well known members who were present. Scanning down the names, I can picture the happy scenes — the laughing, joking, and good humour around the tables. Yet, there is a tinge of sadness too, for a great many of the names I knew so well, just like Owd Tom, have now passed on.

How well I recall the year of 1966, when returning from a cycle ride on a sunny summer afternoon, I called by chance at the Lower Rivington Barn for a mug of tea and cake, before I made my way homewards. A meeting of the Autumn Tints was just ending, and I knew many there. Then, walking towards me was Ben Booth, his face beaming with pleasure. I feel sure someone must have told him I had attained the age of 50.

"How old are you, Albert?" he asked. "Fifty!" I replied. "Right, you're in . . . Welcome to the Autumn Tints". Shortly afterwards I received a badge of membership with my name engraved on the 'scroll' and just below those intertwined initials of Tom Hughes. I have worn it with pride ever since. I shall always give thanks to dear old Ben Booth for having enrolled me on attaining my '50th cycling milestone'.

Ben Booth was to continue as Secretary until 1973, when his untimely death was a deep shock to all Autumn Tint members who knew and respected him so well.

In all sports and pastimes, there are men and women who have their aims and ambitions, to experience the glow of a long achievement, and to stand as a satisfied memory in one's 'veteran' years.

With Ben Booth, it was to cycle from Lands End to John o'Groats, not as a record attempt, but as a personal goal to look back upon. Unhappily he did not enjoy the best of health, but decided to attempt his 'dream' in two stages — Land's End to his home, and then to and from John o'Groats back to his home.

Alas, within 50 miles of his John o'Groats' accomplishment he suffered a heart attack and was conveyed to hospital in Inverness, and then conveyed home where he died shortly afterwards. He was 67 years of age.

I have before me, as I write, the copy of a poem composed by one of his companion members W. Bell, that relates the sad story, of an ambition that fate robbed Ben of:

OUR BEN

A cherished highlight of the "Autumn Tints",
We heard the news with bated breath,
His cycling comrades all were stunned,
Saddened by his untimely death.

Yet even in our sorrowing,
Memories most precious do arise,
of happy 'meets' with him we shared;
With quiet thanks our hearts are stirred.

Old soldiers never die, they say,
Nor thought of Ben o'er fade away.
Fair deeds — not words, life's lessons teach;
Ben practised — never did he preach!

For perfect Secretary then,
No further look than "Our Ben"
We wonder who can take his place
With such efficiency and grace.

Industry robbed him of good health;
Yet in spite of frailty, age and pain,
In firm belief that nature heals,
Sought health in nature on two wheels.

Of all the cures men can devise
There's none to equal nature's tray
Right food, fresh air, and exercise,
Ben found in cycling the best way.

And hoping to prolong his days
Ben turned to nature and her ways
Spite of industries knavish tricks
Attained the age of Sixty-six!

"A gentleman of the road". Tom Higham was Secretary of The Autumn Tints Cycling Comrades for 19 years, up to 1990.

To cover this fair isle of ours
From end to end — the cyclist's dream,
Home from Land's End, there and back,
Ben bravely took the Northern track.

Alas for Ben! 'twas not to be!
With only fifty miles to run,
His strength gave out — was conveyed home,
It seemed his cycling days were done.

— And done indeed they were! Next day,
Ben took the "Road around the Bend!"
The goal he reached awaits us all —
Not John O'Groats — Life's Journey's End!

Ben took the path that seemed his best;
And now he takes his well-earned rest,
His ashes lie in sacred urn,
And we are left his loss to mourn.

We members of the "Autumn Tints"
Will ne'er forget 'tis certain then,
Though handicapped yet without stints,
The Selfless Service of "Our Ben".

There were, naturally, many who declared that Ben was foolish to have attempted such a Herculean task and member W. Bell continued the sad story with another poem in different style to 'silence them'.

Don't grumbling say "He shouldn't ha' done it"
Admire instead his gallant spirit.
His fateful effort don't condemn,
Don't label him "An Also Ran".
None knows how soon our time may come
When we may finish life's short run.
We all have secret cherished hopes,
something we intend one day to do;
Intention firm that we one day
Will make our lifetime's dream come true.
Perhaps we will — with luck we may,
Maybe like Ben, things won't work out
In just our cherished, hoped-for-way.

To try as Ben did 'tis not a sin
And Ben was not one to give in.
His gallant effort came to an end
With John O'Groats's just round the bend.
Ben took the road that seemed his best,
That lead him to his well-earned rest.
His gallant effort came to a close;
His courage like a beacon glows,
And gleams gem-like in each heart,
Of "Autumn Tints" — in every part.
His fine example doth inspire,
And warm our hearts as by a fire.
Alas! "Our Ben's" no more! What then?
The future lies beyond our ken.
We wonder sadly where and when
We'll get another like "Our Ben!"
In spite of illness — without stints,
Ben gave his best to the "Autumn Tints".
We bow in silent admiration,
His courage and determination,
Has left in memories golden store,
A radiant glow for ever more!

It has been remarkable that in the history of the 'Autumn Tints Cycling Comrades' from its foundation in 1924, there had only been three previous Secretaries, up to Tom Higham's appointment.

Tom Higham with his calm serene manner, and with a natural flair for organising things was to give so generously his time to keep up the aims and traditions of the Tints. At each meet he was there to make the event so enjoyable to all . . . the opening welcome to the members, the reading of letters and correspondence from absent friends, and the sympathetic messages to those suffering from ill-health, and he was there on behalf of the Tints to pay respect to those who had unhappily passed away. The very essence of friendship and comradeship began by Owd Tom in 1924 had never been stronger.

With advancing age, Tom's health began to suffer and in 1990 he reluctantly had to announce his retirement from the Secretaryship.

Unknown to him, a 'secret' fund had been opened, and generously contributed to by the members, to provide a fitting 'testimonial' in gratitude for his services. The presentation took place on the occasion of the 1990 Annual Dinner at the Rivington Hall Barn.

Just as Owd Tom Hughes had received an illuminated address on the occasion of his 70th birthday, so was Tom Higham to be honoured by a similar one, brilliantly and expertly executed by Liverpool member H.S. Williams. The wording, keeping to the tradition and style of those chosen for Owd Tom's, also included the delightful verse of Thomas Moore's poem . . . for after all, all men are young in heart:

> Presented to Mr. Thomas Higham "Tommy"
> By the Members of
> The Autumn Tints Cycling Comrades
> as a slight token of their appreciation and sincere thanks —
> and of their love and esteem for him for all he has done for
> the club over the years, with the hope that he may long
> continue to be an Outstanding Example of what consistent
> cycling will do to keep a man fit and enable him to get the
> best out of life.
> "Snow may o'er his head be flung
> But his heart — his heart is young"
> Tom Moore

A clock containing a suitably engraved plate and including the symbolic club badge, was also presented.

The event and presentation attracted the attention of the Press, with a report and photograph appearing in the newspaper the following week.

In these final pages of my story, it is good to know that the 'Autumn Tints Cycling Comrades' continues to maintain its place of honour in the English cycling scene and that the Secretaryship is currently in the capable hands of Ron Liptrot of Uppermill, Oldham, who is following on the good work of those who have served so well in the past.

Ron has been Secretary since December 1990, and is a sprightly 63-years-old (at the time of writing), and has been an enthusiastic cyclist since he acquired his first machine when 11-years-old.

Each and every year, the annual programme is distributed to members, and certainly makes interesting reading. Mentioned are the popular sections . . . the East and West Pennines, Calderdale and Craven, Nottingham, Derbyshire and Lincolnshire, Teeside and East Anglia. Most important are the names of members who have attained the 'Seniority' status of 70 years of age, with their ages and months of birthdays.

Though sadly gone forever are the days of the old 'Unicorn' memories at Walton-le-Dale, with those huge mouth-watering birthday cakes, when up to a hundred could be present — that lovely spirit fostered from the first early years is still very much in evidence.

From that summer's day of July 12th, 1924, when Owd Tom in his wisdom founded the Tints, there have been those members who have expressed their inner feelings of thankfulness in many ways — by dedicated service, the maintaining of friendships and companionship in times of sickness, as well as the comfort displayed when the last farewells of respect have had to be expressed.

* * * *

Perhaps many of you reading this story, will not have heard about Charles Lee of Warrington, a member around the years 1959-60. He conveyed the feeling of cycling magic, especially in the twilight shadows of one's 'Autumn' years to perfection in a delightful poem.

I am sure if Owd Tom had been alive to have read it, it would have brought the tears to his eyes:

LIFE'S TWILIGHT SHADOWS

The hills are green in the early light,
When morning treads on the skirts of night,
The hills are grey when the sun's gone west,
'Tis then the wheelmen love them best.

Men we are told are like the grass
And that is the reason it comes to pass
That mortals change in a life's long day
From the young and green to the old and grey.

Not so long since it seems to me,
I was as speedy as youth could be,
Cycling the highways as young folk do,
'Neath skies quite grey, and skies quite blue.

But now this head of mine looks strange
For silver threads have wrought a change,
I seem to have pedalled the swiftest way,
From the young and green, to the old and grey.

My life has been a pleasant thing
In winter and summer, autumn and spring,
Days in December, end days in June
Seem to have ended much too soon.

Twilight shadows are closing in,
I notice them after every spin,
But I'm pleased to have cycled o'er life's rough way,
From the young and green, to the old and grey.

POSTSCRIPT:

Tommy Higham had greeted with enthusiasm my writing of this book about Owd Tom Hughes, and had fully supported my desire to perpetuate his memory; it was also his ambition to see it published. Alas, it was not to be.

Tommy died on 20th April 1992 (Easter Monday) aged 77 years.

I shall always be indebted to him for the valuable help, patience and assistance he gave to me during the preparation of the book. His passing will also be a great loss to the 'Autumn Tints Cycling Comrades', but his name like that of Owd Tom's, will always be revered, by those of us who knew him so well.

As his obituary stated, and I am sure everyone who knew him will agree: "He was a gentleman of the road".

11

A 'Meet'
With The 'Tints'

IN this chapter I will endeavour to convey the meaning — the link with the nature-loving cyclist on his way to a meeting of the 'Tints' at a popular haunt, and the happiness experienced there.

Tucked away at the head of a little dingle, and backing a meadow threaded by once ancient mill streams, are the Millcroft Tea Gardens at Norden, some four miles north-west of Rochdale.

A hundred years of history is enshrined here — some 80 of them in catering so well for the thousands of cyclists and outdoor lovers, who have been endeared to the tranquility of the spot.

There are not many 'tea houses' like this left in England today, and when you are there, that feeling of lovely nostalgia we 'old timers' associate with the golden years of cycling is captured to perfection.

You find it in the glass-fronted shed that adjoins the old house, that serves as the tea room, you find it in the traditional trestle tables, fascinating furniture, and the age-old harmonium, all visible links with yesterday.

Best of all, however, is the feeling of happiness that radiates, and the spell of friendship that always prevails there.

Here, the cycling 'old timers' of the 'Autumn Tints Cycling

The Millcroft Tea Gardens at Norden, near Rochdale, one of the favourite North West haunts of the Autumn Tints Cycling Comrades.

Comrades' meet at regular intervals. For their 'meets' and get-togethers there can be no finer venue.

If, therefore, I have perhaps aroused your curiosity, and have attained the age of 50, or if you are approaching that 'milestone' of your life, and are wondering what 'Millcroft' or the 'Autumn Tints' is all about, why not join me throughout the ensuing paragraphs of this chapter and I will take you there. I am sure you will enjoy a most unique experience.

Now, there are several ways of approaching Norden, and it is well signposted with easy access from Rochdale. Not liking the highways, I have my own special way of approach; a lovely meander along little lanes, spiced with an equally little spell of 'rough stuff' to tingle my adventure blood, to take me there by the 'tradesmens' entrance' as it were.

After the short distance from my Lancashire home town to Bury, I pedal the few miles along the Rochdale Old Road (B6222) to Hooley Bridge, and here I swing sharply left to a little area of deep stream and brook valleys and dells.

'Ashworth Road' says the sign at the bridge, and immediately I am out of the saddle, as a steep climb is before me, tree enshrouded, and with generous woodlands deep on my left below. I am content to walk for it is so lovely and quiet. It was not always so. The Ashworth Valley once hummed with activity; taking advantage of the many streams and brooks, mills were constructed with great waterwheels to power them. Of late years, with 'conservation' to the fore, sterling work has been done in a vast 'tidy up' to preserve such interesting links with our ancient industrial heritage.

Topping the hill, I am able to ride again, and the fields and hedgerows appear, and there are sweeping views to distant Lancashire contours. Cattle graze the meadows to give that atmosphere and touch of pastoral quietude. I am now close to Ashworth itself, a trim little place telling of the fusion between the present and yesterday. There are no harsh red bricks here to mar the pattern and appeal of old mellow stone, and all the dwellings seemingly speak of snug and cosy interiors. I linger for a few moments in the rural peace of the surroundings, and cast an appreciative eye at the door of Ashworth Hall, still retaining the heavy 'studs' favoured by landlords of the past.

Beyond the village, I turn at School Row, passing the 'Tom Thumb' building that formerly served as the school, and then as the road prepares to dip towards another stream valley, I welcome with pleasure the leafy bridleway that will take me above a wooded dell.

I like this little bridleway ... so befitting its name, for here and there are still traces of paved portions, from the days when horse traffic held sway. There is a final dip down towards the stream level and in a clearing are the remains of a once large mill. Walls have been rebuilt, water sluices cleared and cleaned, and seats and tables have been provided to make a first-class picnic spot. The high-towering mill chimney has been retained to keep a sentinel-like eye on things.

There is the noisy chatter of water everywhere, and familiar flowers that favour the damp places, garland the surrounding dell, as I negotiate with the bike up the flight of rustic steps (more conservation work), and these take me to the meadow beyond. A stile gives entrance to the pathway hugging the verge of the dell, to end at a stout field gate, stile, and cattle-grid, and within yards, I am in Monkey Tree Lane, leading to the head of the little dingle I have mentioned, with Millcroft sitting there at its head.

Why Monkey Tree Lane you might ask? Well, 90 years ago, a past owner of Millcroft planted 28 monkey trees. Today they are like veritable 'Methuselahs', with octopus-like tentacles.

How I always appreciate the first glimpse of Millcroft peeping through the trees. The once old farmhouse holding the spell of its hey-deys in a calm serene manner. Many Autumn Tint members will already have arrived and there will be bikes a'plenty outside, parked by what are ancient school seats. I love this arrival and to greet old friends from many towns, who gather here for the monthly 'meet'. I also meet and make the acquaintance of new members, giving a warm handshake to new 'old timers' who have just reached this 50th milestone of their cycling lives, and have joined us on the threshold of their veteran years. One is never a stranger for long at Millcroft, for cycling hospitality is renowned and any newcomer is quickly made welcome.

From the kitchen, there is regular 'coming-and-going' from Mr. Kenneth Leach the proprietor and his band of helpers, all bearing trays of traditional Lancashire pint pots of tea, and favourite cycling dishes.

At Millcroft you can either eat your own sandwiches or take your choice from the wide selection offered on the menu. Millcroft quickly fills as more and more Tint members arrive; everyone seems to be chattering away 'fifty to the dozen'. It does my heart good to see and hear it all and to be a part of it.

I sit over my pint mug of tea, chatting to three Tint members who have also cycled here; they are 82, 80 and 76 respectively. Other members and friends from several Lancashire and Yorkshire towns are here too. Two new members beaming with pleasure are joining in the congenial atmosphere. No matter that there are many bald heads, grey and thinning hair and wrinkles befitting advancing years — this is cycling friendship at its best. A merry twinkle in the eyes, that keen zest for living and relishing the joys and delights of being awheel, to cherish the good but simple pleasures that contribute much to the blessings of one's 'autumn' years.

There is a lull in the chatter; a polite request for silence as the Secretary opens the meeting. He bids the traditional welcome to everyone. Correspondence and letters are read from absent members in all parts and news obtained of members suffering from the infirmities of advancing age, and of those who have had to curtail their cycling activities. As always, the good wishes of the 'Tints' will be conveyed to them. Sadly, and often on these occasions, there has to be moments of condolence, as we realise we have had to say the last 'goodbyes' to names we have known, and respected over the years.

'Birthdays' then follow. The Secretary reads out the names and ages of members over 70, whose birthdays occur during the month, and should that member be present, he or she is given an ovation, and invited to say a few words. The age 'milestone' of 70 denotes, as Owd Tom decreed, that 'Senior' membership of the Autumn Tints had now been bestowed on the member. There is now a large following of lady members, who in these their own 'veteran' years, do not shy away from revealing their ages — so different from their younger years!

As always, the meeting ends with a big 'thank you' to Kenneth Leach the proprietor of Millcroft and his band of helpers for offering once again such appreciated hospitality.

Millcroft now begins to empty; there is lingering outside, the packing of saddlebags, the farewells and handshakes, then bikes are wheeled away as once again Tint members make their way homewards.

I leisurely pedal my own homeward way, thoroughly pleased with the events of the past few hours. I am now in my contemplative mood, experiencing that feeling and satisfied happiness for the life of cycling I lead, and to be a member of this unique club.

This morning I have followed the little lanes by the forest glades and meadows, and I have sensed the beauty and joy of the journey. I have been in the company of the good friends and comrades of the Autumn Tints.

It has been a perfect day.

I am sure that if Owd Tom Hughes could have been with me, he would have given a contented nod of his head, and there would have been a twinkle in the eyes of that nut brown face, in the knowledge that what he had created had a rosy future and that "everything was still reight gradely".

12

The Chair
of Memories

IN every club and organisation, there have been those who over the years, have given sterling service in an official capacity. It is fitting that there has also been many differing ways of honouring them, so that their names remain 'evergreen'.

Perhaps it might be in the form of a testimonial, a plaque on a wall, a silver cup to be competed for annually, or a seat in a particular favourite spot in the countryside.

The 'Autumn Tints Cycling Comrades' are fortunate to possess a rare treasure to honour their past officials . . . a lovely, well shaped and lovely-proportioned ladder-backed rush-seated antique chair. Known as 'The Tom Hughes Chair', it is a symbol of esteem, and a lasting reminder of the names of past officials whose names are still cherished. For their names are engraved on the chair for all to see.

The story of the Chair had its beginnings at a past meeting of the Tints, at the Unicorn many years ago, and I have been indebted to Mr. George Fletcher, who was the last proprietor for acquainting me with the details.

Mr. Fred Fletcher (the father of George) was consulted about the purchase of a chair, and being something of an expert in

*Tom Higham, late Autumn Tints Veteran, gives 'The Tom Hughes Chair'
a dusting before a 'Meet' at Rivington, near Bolton.*

antiques, he arranged the purchase from a well known establishment in Preston. The chair quickly became a firm favourite, being used for the meetings and quite naturally it became 'The Tom Hughes Chair', as his would be the first name to be remembered by it.

The Chair remained at the Unicorn until its closure, when it was taken to Rivington Hall, near Bolton, where it now occupies pride of place on the occasions of the Annual Dinner held in the Rivington Hall Barn.

The inscription that heads the names on the Chair reads:

> In Memoria Nostra Vivit 1866 — Tom Hughes — 1950
> Founder of the "Autumn Tints" Cycling Comrades 1924.

The Chair is maintained in tip-top condition and polished with loving care each week by the good people of Rivington Hall Barns.

In its way, the Chair so silently, yet so eloquently, records the fascinating story of the Tints, and those who have served so well.

13

The Finale

MY calling at the home of Owd Tom's grandson at Standish, near Wigan, resulted in his arranging for me to call on Owd Tom's eldest grand-daughter — 80-years-old Mrs. Edna Cottam of Whitley, Wigan.

I was received with typical Lancashire hospitality. There were many family photographs to look at, all of which she had carefully prepared for my visit.

All the photographs radiated the happiness in keeping with the large families of years ago, and on most of them Owd Tom was there, his face usually creased with laughter. Perhaps there was a tinge of regret on one or two of them, as Owd Tom was seen with a walking stick. Mrs. Cottam then related the story of his cycling accident in Wales.

There were several wedding photographs. "Oh yes ... he came to all the weddings," said Mrs. Cottam. I remarked that on some photographs, he was wearing a cap. "Yes, but he was losing his hair, you see!", she said.

Early photographs were produced of groups of the Autumn Tints at several favourite venues, with Owd Tom always to the fore . . . but then he had to be, for he was an expert with the 'delayed action' function of his camera that gave him valuable seconds to run to the front of the group to be included in the picture.

Eventually with a little sadness in her voice, Mrs. Cottam told me of her grandad's last days; of how Owd Tom, after a lifetime of cycling and being out-doors, could not adapt to living alternately with two of his daughters as claustrophobia and frustration began to affect him. On one occasion he had smashed the large front window of his room, and the unhappy day was to come when he had to be admitted to the Billinge Hospital. His memory was failing fast. Often he was bewildered and did not know where he was.

The sad end came on Thursday morning, January 5th, 1950. He was 83.

There was a fitting obituary published the following Saturday in the *Wigan Observer and District Advertiser:*

DEATH OF "OWD TOM" HUGHES
A LIFETIME OF CYCLING

Mr. Tom Hughes, the Veteran Cyclist whose home was in Birch Street, Wigan, died at Billinge Hospital on Thursday morning where he had been a patient for some time. Mr. Hughes passed away peacefully. He was in his 84th year.

Mr. Hughes, well known as "Owd Tom", was probably the country's most famous cyclist. His mileages were colossal, and it is conservatively estimated that his total mileage during his lifetime of cycling must have exceeded 400,000 miles, and he regularly topped 10,000 miles a year.

A small lean man with close cropped grey hair, a nut brown face, Mr. Hughes cycled all over the British Isles, and his friends in the cycling world were legion. In addition to riding his cycle about his native land, Mr. Hughes visited probably every European and Scandinavian country. He thought nothing of packing his rucksack and getting astride his bicycle, and riding off to say Oberammergau, the village near Munich famous for its decentennial Passion Play.

But most of all, Mr. Hughes loved England, and he was never happier than when visiting its beauty spots, many of which, indeed, were so remote that they could only be reached by a man afoot or awheel on a bicycle. From this it must not be thought that Mr. Hughes was a work-shy man. For instance in 1925, when he cycled 9981 miles, he also found time to work 375 shifts in the coal mine an average paradoxically enough of over seven days per week for the whole of the year.

Mr. Hughes often compiled his remarkable mileages by cycling great distances at the week-end, and there were years when this remarkable man never sat down to a Sunday's dinner at home. Mr. Hughes had seen the evolution of the bicycle in practical way. He began his cycling career on a "Hobby Horse" a rude machine with open frame, two wheels and handlebars, which Mr. Hughes propelled by pushing it along with his feet. From the "Hobby Horse", Mr. Hughes graduated to a tall Ordinary popularly known as a "Penny- Farthing" which he used to mount by first climbing onto a convenient wall, and then came his "Safety Bicycle" a machine with wheels of unequal size which was driven from pedals on the front wheel. Time passed, and Mr. Hughes acquired his first chain driven machine, but this one still had solid tyres, for it was not until 1910 that Mr. Hughes was to be seen riding a bicycle with pneumatic tyres.

The bicycle then evolved rapidly for thousands were taking to the open road, and in the latter years of his remarkable career, he only gave up cycling when within six months of his 80th birthday. Mr. Hughes was riding the modern "slippered ease roadster", a bicycle about 22 lbs in weight and light steel frame, hiduminium fittings and handlebars and low gears.

"The Secret of Cycling". . . These are the words of Mr. Hughes "The correct way of dealing with declining powers, is to adjust pace to distance, so that these are brought within cyclists' ability. Another important point is to have a suitable mount, a light bicycle is most important".

Mr. Hughes was the Founder of the famous Autumn Tints Cycling Club, and it may well be that this unique club will provide his epitaph. The club was founded some years ago and to qualify as an Autumn Tint, a cyclist had to be 50 years of age or over, and each member who attained his 70th birthday awheel was invariably entertained with a birthday party given at the Unicorn Cafe, a roadhouse cafe at Walton-le-Dale, that was a well known inn in coaching days.

Cyclists from all over the country rode to these birthday gatherings, which acquired such publicity that at one party newsreels cameramen were present to film proceedings. Mr. Hughes was predeceased by his wife, and he leaves two sons and four daughters. The funeral takes place on Tuesday next. A service at St. John's Church, Pemberton at 3 p.m. will precede the internment in the churchyard.

Having read Owd Tom's obituary from the records of the *Wigan Observer and District Advertiser*, I could not write a 'Finale until, as a Veteran Autumn Tint member myself, I had paid my respects to his memory, before his grave.

His grand-daughter Mrs. Edna Cottam, who had told me of Tom's last days, had given me directions. The churchyard of St. John's Church, Pemberton, near Wigan, was deserted on the bitterly cold winter's day I decided to visit his grave. With me, were two Junior members of the Autumn Tints, who had expressed a desire to accompany me. We spoke in hushed voices as we wheeled the bicycles through the churchyard.

All around was evidence of the final chapter of life that will one day come to all of us. 'Neath each and every stone, there is a story of the 'play of life'.

Master poet Shakespeare captured it all to perfection in a dramatic verse that takes its place in our 'golden treasury' of literature:

> "All the world's a stage
> And all men and women merely players:
> They have their exits and their entrances,
> And one man in his time plays many parts".

To those then who knew and respected Owd Tom Hughes, most certainly his name will live on in the annals of cycling, and equally to those who only know of him by name and his intertwined initials on the badge of the Autumn Tints Cycling Comrades which he created.

It was, therefore, with a feeling of great happiness, I stood with my two companions before his grave with our bicycles. There was a tinge of sadness to see that his stone had been broken . . but displayed intact was the name of his good wife who had pre-deceased him, and his own:

Alice Ann Hughes   *Thomas (Owd Tom) Hughes*

IN LOVING MEMORY OF
ALICE ANN
BELOVED WIFE OF
TOM HUGHES
Who died Feb 17th 1928
Aged 61 years
Also TOM HUGHES husband
of the above who died
5th Jan 1950. Aged 83 years.

* * * *

The little task of pleasure my humble pen had been given was almost at an end. The last 'milestone' along the way was in sight. In my mind's eye, I was being rewarded by a happy picture of Owd Tom Hughes, his nut brown face beaming with pleasure as he pedalled through the meadows of a heavenly Arcadia. Then he stopped to lean on his handlebars, and said to me: "IF YOUR FACE WANTS TO SMILE LET IT. IF NOT, MAKE IT". Then he pedalled off with that gleam of laughter in his eyes.

IF YOUR FACE WANTS TO SMILE.
LET IT. IF NOT. MAKE IT.

SOME NOTES AND HINTS ON RIDING THE 'PENNY-FARTHING' BICYCLE
by Tom Hughes
(Ex-cycle dealer and grandson of 'Owd Tom' Hughes).

PENNY-FARTHING bicycles were made with different diameters of front wheel. A larger diameter of wheel gave a higher gear, in that one revolution of the pedals moved the bicycle further forward than one revolution with a smaller diameter wheel. For example, a 54" diameter wheel would move forward approximately 170" with one complete turn of the pedals, whilst a 48" diameter wheel would only move forward approximately 150". For racing, a rider with long legs had, therefore, a distinct advantage over a rider with shorter legs.

As my grandfather's height was about 5 ft. 5 ins., the length of his legs dictated the diameter of wheel to be no greater than 52", thus putting him somewhat at a disadvantage as a 'racer'.

Riding a Penny-Farthing was a rather tricky business. A fairly upright posture had to be maintained because if one leant too far forward over the handlebars, the centre of gravity of the rider and machine would be moved forward and if this was in front of the hub of the wheel, the rear wheel would leave the ground and the rider would end up over the handlebars.

Mounting a Penny-Farthing was reasonably easy. The rider had to stand behind the cycle and take hold of the handlebars, the left foot was placed on a step part way up the frame tube on the left side and the cycle was started by pushing on the ground — scooter fashion — with the right foot. When the machine was moving, the rider stood upright on the step and lifted his right leg as high as possible so that he could sit on the saddle and then the left leg was brought forward from the step to the left-hand pedal. Alternatively, if the step was affixed to the right- hand side of the frame tube, the right foot was first placed on the step and the same procedure followed through.

Dismounting was much more difficult. A Penny-Farthing had a fixed wheel so that when the wheel was turning, the pedals would also be turning. Just as the left side pedal passed bottom dead centre, the right leg had to be thrown upwards and backwards over the cycle and onto the ground on the left hand side of the machine, just as with a modern cycle, but one had to be quick enough to do this before the left hand pedal reached top dead centre otherwise, the rear wheel would lift off the ground and the rider would be thrown over the handlebars.

In the age of the computer and ever-faster methods of communication and transport, leisurely cycling and interest in bicycling history has never been greater. For those who would like to see collections of early bicycles, listed below are places you can visit. Some of the collections display bicycle collections exclusively, whilst others display bicycles alongside other forms of early road transport. The list does not claim to be complete and it is advisable to check dates of opening and opening times when you are in the area.

ENGLAND:

AVON, Bristol. Bristol Industrial Museum.

CORNWALL, Camelford. Museum of Historic Cycling, The Old Station.

CUMBRIA, Grange-over-Sands. Lakeland Motor Museum, Cark-in- Cartmel.

DEVON, Ilfracombe. Watermouth Castle, Berrynarbor.

DORSET, Christchurch. Christchurch Tricycle Museum.

ESSEX, Harlow. Mark Hall Cycle Museum, First Avenue, Muskham Road.

HAMPSHIRE, Brockenhurst. National Motor Museum, John Montague Building, Beaulieu.

HUMBERSIDE, Hull. 'Streetlife'. Hull Museum of Transport, High Street.

LINCOLNSHIRE, Lincoln. The National Cycle Museum, Brayford Wharf North.

NOTTINGHAMSHIRE, Nottingham. Industrial Museum, Courtyard Buildings, Wollaton Park.

OXFORDSHIRE, Oxford. Benson Veteran Museum, The Bungalow, 61 Brook Street, Benson.

SHROPSHIRE, Oswestry. Oswestry Cycle Museum, Oswald Road.

WARWICKSHIRE, Nuneaton. Arbury Hall.

WEST MIDLANDS, Birmingham. Museum of British Road Transport, St. Agnes Lane, Hale Street.

WEST YORKSHIRE, Hebden Bridge, Automobilia Transport Museum and Inheritance Car Hire, Billy Lane, Old Town, Wadsworth.

SCOTLAND:

BORDERS, Melrose. Melrose Motor Museum, Annay Road.

CLYDE, Glasgow. Museum of Transport, Kelvin Hall, 1 Bunhouse Road, Kelvin Bridge.

DUMFRIES AND GALLOWAY, Dumfries. Dumfries Museum, The Observatory.

LOTHIAN, Longniddry. Aberlady.

WALES:

DYFED, Haverfordwest. Motor Mania and Leisure Park.

GWENT, Usk. Gwent Rural Life Museum, The Malt Barn, New Market Street.